What's the Issue?

WHAT'S RACISM?

By Amy B. Rogers

Published in 2018 by
KidHaven Publishing, an Imprint of Greenhaven Publishing, LLC
353 3rd Avenue
Suite 255
New York, NY 10010

Designer: Deanna Paternostro
Editor: Katie Kawa

Photo Credits: Cover (top) vasara/Shutterstock.com; cover (bottom) © istockphoto.com/VLIET; p. 4 iofoto/Shutterstock.com; pp. 5, 6, 7, 21 Rawpixel.com/Shutterstock.com; pp. 8–9 Maria Kazanova/ Shutterstock.com; p. 10 Sergei Bachlakov/Shutterstock.com; p. 11 Para/Wikimedia Commons; p. 12 Andy Dean Photography/Shutterstock.com; p. 13 ESB Professional/Shutterstock.com; p. 14 mark reinstein/Shutterstock.com; p. 15 Stephen Maturen/Stringer/Getty Images News/ Getty Images; p. 17 Mat Hayward/Shutterstock.com; p. 19 Joseph Sohm/Shutterstock.com; p. 20 Rido/Shutterstock.com.

Cataloging-in-Publication Data

Names: Rogers, Amy B.
Title: What's racism? / Amy B. Rogers.
Description: New York : KidHaven Publishing, 2018. | Series: What's the issue? | Includes glossary and index.
Identifiers: ISBN 9781534525054 (pbk.) | 9781534524378 (library bound) | ISBN 9781534525061 (6 pack) | ISBN 9781534524385 (ebook)
Subjects: LCSH: Racism–Juvenile literature.
Classification: LCC HT1521.R64 2018 | DDC 305.800973–dc23

Printed in the United States of America

CPSIA compliance information: Batch #CW18KL: For further information contact Greenhaven Publishing LLC, New York, New York at 1-844-317-7404.

Please visit our website, www.greenhavenpublishing.com. For a free color catalog of all our high-quality books, call toll free 1-844-317-7404 or fax 1-844-317-7405.

CONTENTS

The Opposite of Equality

The world would be a boring place if everyone looked the same! However, some people don't like certain groups because they look different. They treat others poorly because they see them as part of a different race, which is a group of people who look alike in certain ways. This unfair way of treating people is called racism.

Racism has hurt people throughout history and still hurts people today. It goes against the idea that everyone should be treated equally. How can you fight against racism? Read on to find out!

One way to fight racism is to treat everyone with kindness and respect.

Facing the Facts

According to a 2016 study, 61 percent of Americans said they believe more work needs to be done to make sure people of all races are treated equally.

Is Race Real?

Racists believe humankind is made up of different races of people, and one race is better than all the others. Scientists have discovered, though, that humans aren't as different as racists think they are.

Racial differences don't actually exist in human **genes**, and there's no one set of **traits** people of one race all share. Race is a way of grouping people that was created by humans. It's not something that separates humans from each other in nature. In fact, all humans are part of the same species, or group of living things.

Humans aren't naturally separated by race. However, racism still exists because some people look for ways to easily group others who they see as different—even if those ways aren't based in facts.

Facing the Facts

In the United States, racism has always worked in favor of white people.

The Dangers of Stereotypes

Where do racist beliefs come from? In many cases, they come from a lack of **experience** with people of different races. Humans look for easy and fast ways to group people together. They often do this using stereotypes, which are ideas about all the people of one group that are often overly simple and sometimes completely untrue.

If people don't take the time to get to know people of different races, they often believe stereotypes about all the members of one race. Learning about others is a key to fighting racism.

Facing the Facts

Scientists have stated that making friends with people from different groups is a good way to move beyond stereotypes.

Words to Know

What's the word?	What does it mean?
discrimination	unfair treatment of people or groups who are different from other people or groups
prejudice	a bad feeling about a person or group that's not based in facts
segregation	the act of setting people apart from each other based on differences
stereotype	an idea that's formed about all the people in one group that's often untrue or only partly true
systemic racism (also known as institutional racism)	the unfair treatment of people of different races by a whole society or government

When people talk about racism, they often use these words. It's important to know what they mean and why they can hurt people.

A Long and Painful History

The United States has a long and painful history of racism. For more than 200 years, white people used racist beliefs about people from Africa to **justify** the practice of slavery. Even after slavery was abolished, or ended, in 1865, racism continued.

The civil rights movement of the 1950s and 1960s worked to fight discrimination against African Americans and segregation in schools, on buses, and in many other places. Although many laws were passed during this time to end these unfair practices, racism didn't go away completely. It's hard to change people's beliefs—even when they're unfair.

Facing the Facts 🔍

White settlers used racist stereotypes about Native Americans to justify taking their lands and treating them poorly.

One of the leaders of the civil rights movement was Dr. Martin Luther King Jr. His most famous speech is called "I Have a Dream," and it was about his dream that people of all races would one day be treated equally in the United States.

11

Prejudice Based in Fear

Other groups have also had to deal with racism in the United States. For example, Asian Americans have dealt with racism ever since Chinese workers were first discriminated against in the 1800s.

In addition, people with **Middle Eastern** roots, also known as Arab Americans, face a certain kind of racism even though they've often been considered white. After the deadly **terrorist** attacks of September 11, 2001, were carried out by men from Middle Eastern countries, many people began to stereotype all Arab Americans as terrorists. This has led to discrimination and even hate crimes against Arab Americans.

Most Arab Americans love America and would never do anything to harm other people. However, some people are afraid of and dislike every person who looks like they come from the Middle East based on the actions of a few bad people.

Facing the Facts

Members of the Latinx community, who have their roots in **Latin American** countries, often face discrimination and prejudice. However, they come from many different racial backgrounds, so the unfair treatment they face isn't **technically** considered racism.

The Fight Continues

In 2008, American voters elected their first African American president, Barack Obama. Some people believed the election of Obama meant the end of racism in the United States. However, that wasn't true.

For example, in August 2017, a large gathering of white supremacists, who believe white people are better than people of all other races, was held in Charlottesville, Virginia. A man then drove his car into a group of people who gathered to speak out against racism. This **violent** event caused many to think more deeply about racism in America.

Facing the Facts

The most well-known white supremacist group in the United States is the Ku Klux Klan (KKK). This group has used acts of racist violence to scare people they see as different, especially African Americans.

After the events that happened in Charlottesville, gatherings were held across the United States for those who wanted to speak out against racism and in favor of equality.

15

Talk About It

Racism is a hard thing for people to talk about. It makes some people uncomfortable, and some people think talking about it only makes the problem worse. They think it's best to **ignore** the problem and act as if race doesn't matter.

However, race still matters for people who deal with racism. Talking about racism helps call attention to struggles that are still **affected** by race. Ignoring the problem of racism only deepens the divide, or gap, between people. Talking openly leads to more understanding, which is one way to fight racism.

Facing the Facts

White privilege is a set of advantages white people have because their race is in a position of power over other races. White people can still face hard times, but racism doesn't play a part in their struggles the way it can for people of other races.

A good way to fight racism is to celebrate differences instead of ignoring them or being afraid of them.

From the NAACP to Black Lives Matter

Many people and groups are working to address the problem of racism in the United States. One group that's famous for fighting against racism is the National Association for the Advancement of Colored People (NAACP). It's the oldest civil rights **organization** in the United States. Today, it's working to end unfair practices to keep people from voting, prejudice in law enforcement, and many other problems black Americans face.

In 2013, a movement called Black Lives Matter started to call attention to violence against black Americans. Black Lives Matter also calls attention to systemic racism and empowers black men and women to fight back against it.

Some people think Black Lives Matter means other lives don't matter. This isn't true. Black Lives Matter means black men, women, and children matter, even though racist ways of thinking and acting make it seem as if they don't have the same value as white people.

Facing the Facts 🔍

A commonly used term for any person who isn't white is person of color. It's sometimes shortened to POC.

Real Problem, Real Solutions

Racism is a big problem that may seem too hard for one person to fight. However, there are small things everyone can do to help fight for equality.

One of the easiest but most important things you can do is get to know people who are different from you. Racism is built on a lack of understanding and respect. Talking openly with many different people about their lives can help people begin to see each other as individuals and not stereotypes. Racism isn't an easy thing to talk about, but facing it is the only way to truly fight it.

Facing the Facts

The number of Americans who believe racism is a big problem in the United States nearly doubled between 2011 and 2017.

WHAT CAN YOU DO?

Listen to people when they talk about the racism they face.

Raise money for groups that fight racism.

Get to know people of different races, and talk openly about your differences and the things you have in common.

Talk to your family about racism.

Understand that racism is still a real problem, and don't ignore it.

If you hear someone saying racist things, tell them it's wrong.

These are just some of the many things everyone can do to fight racism. How will you help make the world a more equal place for people of all races?

GLOSSARY

affect: To produce an effect on something.

experience: Directly seeing or doing things as a way to gain understanding.

genes: The parts of cells considered the building blocks of a living thing that control the appearance, growth, and other qualities of a living thing.

ignore: To refuse to take notice of something.

justify: To prove or show that something is just or right.

Latin America: All the Americas south of the United States.

Middle East: The part of the world made up of the countries of southwestern Asia and northern Africa.

organization: A group formed for a specific purpose.

technical: According to a strict explanation of rules or facts.

terrorist: A person who uses violence and fear as a way to achieve a political goal.

trait: A quality that makes one person or thing different from another.

violent: Relating to the use of bodily force to hurt others.

FOR MORE INFORMATION

WEBSITES

Let's Fight Racism!
www.un.org/en/letsfightracism/
This United Nations website highlights different ways people can speak out against racism on social media and learn more about people of different races.

NAACP
www.naacp.org/
Visitors to this website can learn more about the oldest civil rights organization in the United States and how they can help it continue its work against racism.

BOOKS

Asim, Jabari. *A Child's Introduction to African American History: The Experiences, People, and Events That Shaped Our Country.* New York, NY: Black Dog & Leventhal, 2018.

Mahoney, Emily. *American Civil Rights Movement.* New York, NY: PowerKids Press, 2017.

Ogden, Charlie. *Equality and Diversity.* New York, NY: Crabtree Publishing Company, 2017.

INDEX